# The Country of Marriage

Books by Wendell Berry

*Novels*
Nathan Coulter
A Place on Earth
The Memory of Old Jack

*Poetry*
The Broken Ground
Openings
Findings
Farming: A Hand Book
The Country of Marriage
Clearing

*Essays*
The Long-Legged House
The Hidden Wound
The Unforeseen Wilderness
A Continuous Harmony

# The Country
# of Marriage

WENDELL BERRY

A Harvest/HBJ Book
Harcourt Brace Jovanovich, Publishers
San Diego   New York   London

Printed in the United States of America

Some of the poems in this volume previously appeared in
*Apple, December, The Hudson Review, Kayak, The Lamp
in the Spine, The Nation, The Ohio Review, Pipedream
Press Penny Paper, Place, Sequoia, The Southern Review,
The Whole Earth Catalogue,* and *The University of
Windsor Review.* "Prayer after Eating," "Anger Against
Beasts," and "A Homecoming" were first published in
*Poetry;* "The Wild Geese" in *Esquire.*

Library of Congress Cataloging in Publication Data

Berry, Wendell, 1934-
    The country of marriage.

(A Harvest/HBJ book)
I. Title.
[PS3552.E75C64 1975]    811'.5'4    75-5941
ISBN 0-15-622697-9

First Harvest/HBJ edition 1975
  D  E  F  G  H  I  J

*For Tanya*

# Contents

# The Country of Marriage

. . . Except a corn of wheat fall into the
ground and die, it abideth alone. . . .
—John 12:24

# The Old Elm Tree by the River

Shrugging in the flight of its leaves,
it is dying. Death is slowly
standing up in its trunk and branches
like a camouflaged hunter. In the night
I am wakened by one of its branches
crashing down, heavy as a wall, and then
lie sleepless, the world changed.
That is a life I know the country by.
Mine is a life I know the country by.
Willing to live and die, we stand here,
timely and at home, neighborly as two men.
Our place is changing in us as we stand,
and we hold up the weight that will bring us down.
In us the land enacts its history.
When we stood it was beneath us, and was
the strength by which we held to it
and stood, the daylight over it
a mighty blessing we cannot bear for long.

# Poem

Willing to die,
you give up
your will. Keep still
until, moved
by what moves
all else, you move.

# Breaking

Did I believe I had a clear mind?
It was like the water of a river
flowing shallow over the ice. And now
that the rising water has broken
the ice, I see that what I thought
was the light is part of the dark.

# The Country of Marriage

## 1

I dream of you walking at night along the streams
of the country of my birth, warm blooms and the
    nightsongs
of birds opening around you as you walk.
You are holding in your body the dark seed of my
    sleep.

## 2

This comes after silence. Was it something I said
that bound me to you, some mere promise
or, worse, the fear of loneliness and death?
A man lost in the woods in the dark, I stood
still and said nothing. And then there rose in me,
like the earth's empowering brew rising
in root and branch, the words of a dream of you
I did not know I had dreamed. I was a wanderer
who feels the solace of his native land
under his feet again and moving in his blood.
I went on, blind and faithful. Where I stepped
my track was there to steady me. It was no abyss
that lay before me, but only the level ground.

3

Sometimes our life reminds me
of a forest in which there is a graceful clearing
and in that opening a house,
an orchard and garden,
comfortable shades, and flowers
red and yellow in the sun, a pattern
made in the light for the light to return to.
The forest is mostly dark, its ways
to be made anew day after day, the dark
richer than the light and more blessed
provided we stay brave
enough to keep on going in.


4

How many times have I come into you out of my
        head
with joy, if ever a man was,
for to approach you I have given up the light
and all directions. I come to you
lost, wholly trusting, as a man who goes
into the forest unarmed. It is as though I descend
slowly earthward out of the air. I rest in peace
in you, when I arrive at last.

## 5

Our bond is no little economy based on the exchange
of my love and work for yours, so much for so much
of an expendable fund. We don't know what its
     limits are—
that puts it in the dark. We are more together
than we know, how else could we keep on
     discovering
we are more together than we thought?
You are the known way leading always to the
     unknown,
and you are the known place to which the unknown
     is always
leading me back. More blessed in you than I know,
I possess nothing worthy to give you, nothing
not belittled by my saying that I possess it.
Even an hour of love is a moral predicament, a
     blessing
a man may be hard up to be worthy of. He can only
accept it, as a plant accepts from all the bounty of the
     light
enough to live, and then accepts the dark,
passing unencumbered back to the earth, as I
have fallen time and again from the great strength
of my desire, helpless, into your arms.

## 6

What I am learning to give you is my death
to set you free of me, and me from myself
into the dark and the new light.   Like the water
of a deep stream, love is always too much. We
did not make it. Though we drink till we burst
we cannot have it all, or want it all.
In its abundance it survives our thirst.
In the evening we come down to the shore
to drink our fill, and sleep, while it
flows through the regions of the dark.
It does not hold us, except we keep returning
to its rich waters thirsty. We enter,
willing to die, into the commonwealth of its joy.


## 7

I give you what is unbounded, passing from dark to
	dark,
containing darkness: a night of rain, an early
	morning.
I give you the life I have let live for love of you:
a clump of orange-blooming weeds beside the road,
the young orchard waiting in the snow, our own life
that we have planted in this ground, as I
have planted mine in you. I give you my love for all
beautiful and honest women that you gather to
	yourself
again and again, and satisfy—and this poem,
no more mine than any man's who has loved a
	woman.

# Zero

The river steams in the cold.
Above it the streams
impend, locked like iron
in the frozen hollows. The cold
reaches of the sky
have leapt onto the ground.
But the wren's at home
in the cubic acre of his song.
House and shed and barn
stand up around their lives
like songs. And I
have a persistent music in me,
like water flowing under ice,
that says the warmer days
will come, blossom and leaf
return again. I live in that,
a flimsy enclosure,
but the song's for singing,
not to dread the end.
The end, anyhow, is always here.
It is the climate we sing in.
A man may ease off into it
any time, like a settler,
tired of farming, starting out
silently into the woods.
On a day like this we have
the end in sight. This is zero,
the elemental poverty

of all that was ever born,
in which nothing lives by chance
but only by choosing to
and by knowing how—and by
the excess of desire that rises
above the mind, surrounding
and hovering like a song.

## Prayer after Eating

I have taken in the light
that quickened eye and leaf.
May my brain be bright with praise
of what I eat, in the brief blaze
of motion and of thought.
May I be worthy of my meat.

# Her First Calf

Her fate seizes her and brings her
down. She's heavy with it. It
wrings her. The great weight
is heaved out of her. It eases.
She moves into what she has become,
sure in her fate now
as a fish free in the current.
She turns to the calf who has broken
out of the womb's water and its veil.
He breathes. She licks his wet hair.
He gathers his legs under him
and rises. He stands, and his legs
wobble. After the months
of his pursuit of her, now
they meet face to face.
From the beginnings of the world
his arrival and her welcome
have been prepared. They have always
known each other.

# Kentucky River Junction

*to Ken Kesey & Ken Babbs*

Clumsy at first, fitting together
the years we have been apart,
and the ways.

But as the night
passed and the day came, the first
fine morning of April,

it came clear:
the world that has tried us
and showed us its joy

was our bond
when we said nothing.
And we allowed it to be

with us, the new green
shining.

\*

Our lives, half gone,
stay full of laughter.

Free-hearted men
have the world for words.

Though we have been
apart, we have been together.

*

Trying to sleep, I cannot
take my mind away.
The bright day

shines in my head
like a coin
on the bed of a stream.

*

You left
your welcome.

## Manifesto: The Mad Farmer
## Liberation Front

Love the quick profit, the annual raise,
vacation with pay. Want more
of everything ready made. Be afraid
to know your neighbors and to die.
And you will have a window in your head.
Not even your future will be a mystery
any more. Your mind will be punched in a
    card
and shut away in a little drawer.
When they want you to buy something
they will call you. When they want you
to die for profit they will let you know.
So, friends, every day do something
that won't compute. Love the Lord.
Love the world. Work for nothing.
Take all that you have and be poor.
Love someone who does not deserve it.
Denounce the government and embrace
the flag. Hope to live in that free
republic for which it stands.
Give your approval to all you cannot
understand. Praise ignorance, for what man
has not encountered he has not destroyed.
Ask the questions that have no answers.
Invest in the millennium. Plant sequoias.
Say that your main crop is the forest
that you did not plant,
that you will not live to harvest.

Say that the leaves are harvested
when they have rotted into the mold.
Call that profit. Prophesy such returns.
Put your faith in the two inches of humus
that will build under the trees
every thousand years.
Listen to carrion—put your ear
close, and hear the faint chattering
of the songs that are to come.
Expect the end of the world. Laugh.
Laughter is immeasurable. Be joyful
though you have considered all the facts.
So long as women do not go cheap
for power, please women more than men.
Ask yourself: Will this satisfy
a woman satisfied to bear a child?
Will this disturb the sleep
of a woman near to giving birth?
Go with your love to the fields.
Lie easy in the shade. Rest your head
in her lap. Swear allegiance
to what is nighest your thoughts.
As soon as the generals and the politicos
can predict the motions of your mind,
lose it. Leave it as a sign
to mark the false trail, the way
you didn't go. Be like the fox
who makes more tracks than necessary,
some in the wrong direction.
Practice resurrection.

# A Marriage, an Elegy

They lived long, and were faithful
to the good in each other.
They suffered as their faith required.
Now their union is consummate
in earth, and the earth
is their communion. They enter
the serene gravity of the rain,
the hill's passage to the sea.
After long striving, perfect ease.

# The Arrival

Like a tide it comes in,
wave after wave of foliage and fruit,
the nurtured and the wild,
out of the light to this shore.
In its extravagance we shape
the strenuous outline of enough.

## A Song Sparrow Singing
## in the Fall

Somehow it has all
added up to song—
earth, air, rain and light,
the labor and the heat,
the mortality of the young.
I will go free of other
singing, I will go
into the silence
of my songs, to hear
this song clearly.

# The Mad Farmer Manifesto:
# The First Amendment

I

> ". . . it is not too soon to provide by every
> possible means that as few as possible shall be
> without a little portion of land. The small
> landholders are the most precious part of a state."
> —Jefferson, to Reverend James Madison,
> October 28, 1785

That is the glimmering vein
of our sanity, dividing
from us from the start: land
under us to steady us when we stood,
free men in the great communion
of the free. The vision keeps
lighting in my mind, a window
on the horizon in the dark.

II

To be sane in a mad time
is bad for the brain, worse
for the heart. The world
is a holy vision, had we clarity
to see it—a clarity that men
depend on men to make.

## III

It is *ignorant* money I declare
myself free from, money fat
and dreaming in its sums, driving
us into the streets of absence,
stranding the pasture trees
in the deserted language of banks.


## IV

And I declare myself free
from ignorant love. You easy lovers
and forgivers of mankind, stand back!
I will love you at a distance,
and not because you deserve it.
My love must be discriminate
or fail to bear its weight.

# Planting Trees

In the mating of trees,
the pollen grain entering invisible
the domed room of the winds, survives
the ghost of the old forest
that was here when we came. The ground
invites it, and it will not be gone.
I become the familiar of that ghost
and its ally, carrying in a bucket
twenty trees smaller than weeds,
and I plant them along the way
of the departure of the ancient host.
I return to the ground its original music.
It will rise out of the horizon
of the grass, and over the heads
of the weeds, and it will rise over
the horizon of men's heads. As I age
in the world it will rise and spread,
and be for this place horizon
and orison, the voice of its winds.
I have made myself a dream to dream
of its rising, that has gentled my nights.
Let me desire and wish well the life
these trees may live when I
no longer rise in the mornings
to be pleased by the green of them
shining, and their shadows on the ground,
and the sound of the wind in them.

# ιd Geese

ιeback on Sunday morning,
ιvest over, we taste persimmon
ιnd wild grape, sharp sweet
of summer's end. In time's maze
over the fall fields, we name names
that went west from here, names
that rest on graves. We open
a persimmon seed to find the tree
that stands in promise,
pale, in the seed's marrow.
Geese appear high over us,
pass, and the sky closes. Abandon,
as in love or sleep, holds
them to their way, clear,
in the ancient faith: what we need
is here. And we pray, not
for new earth or heaven, but to be
quiet in heart, and in eye
clear. What we need is here.

# The Silence

Though the air is full of singing
my head is loud
with the labor of words.

Though the season is rich
with fruit, my tongue
hungers for the sweet of speech.

Though the beech is golden
I cannot stand beside it
mute, but must say

"It is golden," while the leaves
stir and fall with a sound
that is not a name.

It is in the silence
that my hope is, and my aim.
A song whose lines

I cannot make or sing
sounds men's silence
like a root. Let me say

and not mourn: the world
lives in the death of speech
and sings there.

## Anger Against Beasts

The hook of adrenaline shoves
into the blood. Man's will,
long schooled to kill or have
its way, would drive the beast
against nature, transcend
the impossible in simple fury.
The blow falls like a dead seed.
It is defeat, for beasts
do not pardon, but heal or die
in the absence of the past.
The blow survives in the man.
His triumph is a wound. Spent,
he must wait the slow
unalterable forgiveness of time.

# At a Country Funeral

Now the old ways that have brought us
farther than we remember sink out of sight
as under the treading of many strangers
ignorant of landmarks. Only once in a while
they are cast clear again upon the mind
as at a country funeral where, amid the soft
lights and hothouse flowers, the expensive
solemnity of experts, notes of a polite musician,
persist the usages of old neighborhood.
Friends and kinsmen come and stand and speak,
knowing the extremity they have come to,
one of their own bearing to the earth the last
of his light, his darkness the sun's definitive mark.
They stand and think as they stood and thought
when even the gods were different.
And the organ music, though decorous
as for somebody else's grief, has its source
in the outcry of pain and hope in log churches,
and on naked hillsides by the open grave,
eastward in mountain passes, in tidelands,
and across the sea. How long a time?
Rock of Ages, cleft for me, let me hide my
self in Thee. They came, once in time,
in simple loyalty to their dead, and returned
to the world. The fields and the work
remained to be returned to. Now the entrance
of one of the old ones into the Rock

too often means a lifework perished from the land
without inheritor, and the field goes wild
and the house sits and stares. Or it passes
at cash value into the hands of strangers.
Now the old dead wait in the open coffin
for the blood kin to gather, come home
for one last time, to hear old men
whose tongues bear an essential topography
speak memories doomed to die.
But our memory of ourselves, hard earned,
is one of the land's seeds, as a seed
is the memory of the life of its kind in its place,
to pass on into life the knowledge
of what has died. What we owe the future
is not a new start, for we can only begin
with what has happened. We owe the future
the past, the long knowledge
that is the potency of time to come.
That makes of a man's grave a rich furrow.
The community of knowing in common is the seed
of our life in this place. There is not only
no better possibility, there is no
other, except for chaos and darkness,
the terrible ground of the only possible
new start. And so as the old die and the young
depart, where shall a man go who keeps
the memories of the dead, except home
again, as one would go back after a burial,
faithful to the fields, lest the dead die
a second and more final death.

## The Recognition

You put on my clothes
and it was as though
we met some other place
and I looked and knew
you. This is what we keep
going through, the lyrical
changes, the strangeness
in which I know again
what I have known before.

# Planting Crocuses

## 1

I made an opening
to reach through blind
into time, through
sleep and silence, to new
heat, a new rising,
a yellow flower opening
in the sound of bees.

## 2

Deathly was the giving
of that possibility
to a motion of the world
that would bring it
out, bright, in time.

## 3

My mind pressing in
through the earth's
dark motion toward
bloom, I thought of you,
glad there is no escape.
It is this we will be
turning and re-
turning to.

# Praise

1
Don't think of it.
Vanity is absence.
Be here. Here
is the root and stem
unappraisable
on whose life
your life depends.


2
Be here
like the water
of the hill
that fills each
opening it
comes to, to leave
with a sound
that is a part
of local speech.

# ,hering

,ny age my father
.ld me on his arm
like a hooded bird,
and his father held him so.
Now I grow into brotherhood
with my father as he
with his has grown,
time teaching me
his thoughts in my own.
Now he speaks in me
as when I knew him first,
as his father spoke
in him when he had come
to thirst for the life
of a young son. My son
will know me in himself
when his son sits hooded on
his arm and I have grown
to be brother to all
my fathers, memory
speaking to knowledge,
finally, in my bones.

# A Homecoming

One faith is bondage. Two
are free. In the trust
of old love, cultivation shows
a dark graceful wilderness
at its heart. Wild
in that wilderness, we roam
the distances of our faith,
safe beyond the bounds
of what we know. O love,
open. Show me
my country. Take me home.

## Leaving Home

Whose light is this
that is mine, that
in the shine of the rain
flashes from every leaf
and brightens the rows
where the young stalks
rise, as if bidden
by a knowing woman's hand?
This is no time to go.

The new building stands
unfinished, raw boards
geometric in the air, a man's
design climbing out of the ground
like a tree. When I go
I will carry away its dream.

The light that is mine is not
mine. Were I, like all my kind, to go
and not come back, this light
would return like a faithful woman
until the pent stalk rose
to the shattering of its seed.

No time is a time to go,
and so any time is. Do not wait
to know whose light this is.
Once the heart has felt
the ever-wakening
woman's touch of the light,
there are no more farewells.

# The Mad Farmer's Love Song

O when the world's at peace
and every man is free
then will I go down unto my love

O and I may go down
several times before that.

# The Strangers

The voices of travelers on the hill road
at dusk, calling down to me:
    "Where are we? Where
    does this road go?"
They have followed the ways
by which the country is forgot.
For them, places have changed
into their names, and vanished.
The names rustle in the foliage
by the roadside, furtive
as sparrows. My mind shifts
for whereabouts. Have I found them
in a country they have lost?
Are they lost in a country
I have found? How can they
learn where they are from me,
who have found myself here
after an expense of history
and labor six generations long?
How will they understand my speech
that holds this to be its place
and is conversant with its trees
and stones. We are lost
to each other. I think of changes
that have come without vision
or skill, a new world made
by the collision of particles.
Their blanched faces peer

from their height, waiting
an answer I know too well to speak.
I speak the words they do not know.
I stand like an Indian
before the alien ships.

# The Cruel Plumage

*(A Theme of Edwin Muir)*

All our days are arrows; now at the turn
of life, half-fledged and knowledgeable, I face
the coming of the rest, their grief and pain
made accurate by their joy. So I will learn
the world. Full-feathered, I must fly to an unknown
    place.

# Testament

*And now to the Abbyss I pass*
*Of that Unfathomable Grass . . .*

I

Dear relatives and friends, when my last breath
Grows large and free in the air, don't call it death—
A word to enrich the undertaker and inspire
His surly art of imitating life; conspire
Against him. Say that my body cannot now
Be improved upon; it has no fault to show
To the sly cosmetician. Say that my flesh
Has a perfection in compliance with the grass
Truer than any it could have striven for.
You will recognize the earth in me, as before
I wished to know it in myself: my earth
That has been my care and faithful charge from
    birth,
And toward which all my sorrows were surely
    bound,
And all my hopes. Say that I have found
A good solution, and am on my way
To the roots. And say I have left my native clay
At last, to be a traveler; that too will be so.
Traveler to where? Say you don't know.

## II

But do not let your ignorance
Of my spirit's whereabouts dismay
You, or overwhelm your thoughts.
Be careful not to say

Anything too final. Whatever
Is unsure is possible, and life is bigger
Than flesh. Beyond reach of thought
Let imagination figure

Your hope. That will be generous
To me and to yourselves. Why settle
For some know-it-all's despair
When the dead may dance to the fiddle

Hereafter, for all anybody knows?
And remember that the Heavenly soil
Need not be too rich to please
One who was happy in Port Royal.

I may be already heading back,
A new and better man, toward
That town. The thought's unreasonable,
But so is life, thank the Lord!

III

So treat me, even dead,
As a man who has a place
To go, and something to do.
Don't muck up my face

With wax and powder and rouge
As one would prettify
An unalterable fact
To give bitterness the lie.

Admit the native earth
My body is and will be,
Admit its freedom and
Its changeability.

Dress me in the clothes
I wore in the day's round.
Lay me in a wooden box.
Put the box in the ground.

IV

Beneath this stone a Berry is planted
In his home land, as he wanted.

He has come to the gathering of his kin,
Among whom some were worthy men,

Farmers mostly, who lived by hand,
But one was a cobbler from Ireland,

Another played the eternal fool
By riding on a circus mule

To be remembered in grateful laughter
Longer than the rest. After

Doing what they had to do
They are at ease here. Let all of you

Who yet for pain find force and voice
Look on their peace, and rejoice.

# The Clear Days

*for Allen Tate*

The dogs of indecision
Cross and cross the field of vision.

A cloud, a buzzing fly
Distract the lover's eye.

Until the heart has found
Its native piece of ground

The day withholds its light,
The eye must stray unlit.

The ground's the body's bride,
Who will not be denied.

Not until all is given
Comes the thought of heaven.

When the mind's an empty room
The clear days come.

# To William Butler Yeats

*All that we did, all that we said or sang*
*Must come from contact with the soil, from that*
*Contact everything Antaeus-like grew strong.*
          —"The Municipal Gallery Revisited"

Our kind vandalize the earth,
And yet you give me hope, your truth

The truth of change, and of the soil,
The changer, whose long toil

In summer sun and winter rain
Brings the fallen up again.

When your flesh became a shade,
Annihilated into what it made

And into earth, food for worms,
Substance exfoliating forms,

Poet, you were but keeping faith
With your native truth and place.

Dead, we will come back again
As beasts or worse or better men.

To no truth but change belong
The joy and burden of our song.

# Song

I tell my love in rhyme
In a sentence that must end,
A measurable dividend,
To hold her time against time.

I praise her honest eyes
That keep their beauty clear.
I have nothing to fear
From her, though the world lies,

If I don't lie. Though the hill
Of winter rise, a silent ark,
Our covenant with the dark,
We will speak on until

The flowers fall, and the birds
With their bright songs depart.
Then we will go without art,
Without measure, or words.

# The Asparagus Bed

There is poor pleasure in this
entrance to the ground. A weary
bearing of earth brings the roots
into the dark, from which
tasty shoots will spring.
This work will last, or should,
and one thinks like an ancestor
of the perseverance of delight
life after life—or of the tipped
stalks rising, faithful to the day,
though forgot. And one must think
—it is the trial of the time—
that the ground may be despoiled
and paved to expedite the vain,
the greedy, and the merely bored.
Here, at such risk, the local poet
digs an asparagus bed, one
of the graves of his labor, from which
may there be many resurrections.
Thus the dead escape to life.
But not this year will he know
the fruit of his work. That will come
later, if it thrives, if he lives.
This makes a woman of a man,
laboring to bring forth the new,
in the body's pride and at its cost,
for what good nobody knows.

# Poem for J.

What she made in her body is broken.
Now she has begun to bear it again.
In the house of her son's death
his life is shining in the windows,
for she has elected to bear him again.
She did not bear him for death,
and she does not. She has taken back
into her body the seed, bitter
and joyous, of the life of a man.

In the house of the dead the windows shine
with life. She mourns, for his life was good.
She is not afraid. She is like a field
where the corn is planted, and like the rain
that waters the field, and like the young corn.
In her sorrow she renews life, in her grief
she prepares the return of joy.

She did not bear him for death, and she does not.
There was a life that went out of her to live
on its own, divided, and now she has taken it back.
She is alight with the sudden new life of death.
Perhaps it is the brightness of the dead one
being born again. Perhaps she is planting him,
like corn, in the living and in the earth.
She has taken back into her flesh,
and made light, the dark seed of her pain.

# Inland Passages

## I  *The Long Hunter*

Passed through the dark wall,
set foot in the unknown track,
paths locked in the minds of beasts
and in strange tongues. Footfall
led him where he did not know.
There was a country in the dark where
only blind trust could go.
Some joyous animal paced the woods
ahead of him and filled the air
with steepling song to make a way.
Step by step the darkness bore
the light. The shadow opened
like a pod, and from the height
he saw a place green as welcome
on whose still water the sky lay white.

## II  *The Lover*

As the day goes my mind keeps turning
toward you, making the curve
it loves, going away only to return.
Soon now the dark will come, and I
will go again into the unknown country.
Too long I have been dull and spare
as a winter stem, that bears at last
the warm opening flower of new desire.
It is the return of possibility,
the power to cast away from the known,
that warms me as I turn and look
toward the woods and the distant hills.
The past, the day's dead light, grows
heavy, turning toward new dawn. Again
I can imagine the joyous departure,
the opening of the dark, the going in.

## III  *The Farmer*

I am going with seed
into the beloved body.
Remembering the fields,
I have come through
the dead and the dark,
the winter, the eye
of time, as through
a gap in the hills,
into the new land.

# An Anniversary

What we have been becomes
The country where we are.
Spring goes, summer comes,
And in the heat, as one year
Or a thousand years before,
The fields and woods prepare
The burden of their seed
Out of time's wound, the old
Richness of the fall. Their deed
Is renewal. In the household
Of the woods the past
Is always healing in the light,
The high shiftings of the air.
It stands upon its yield
And thrives. Nothing is lost.
What yields, though in despair,
Opens and rises in the night.
Love binds us to this term
With its yes that is crying
In our marrow to confirm
Life that only lives by dying.
Lovers live by the moon
Whose dark and light are one,
Changing without rest.
The root struts from the seed
In the earth's dark—harvest

And feast at the edge of sleep.
Darkened, we are carried
Out of need, deep
In the country we have married.

5/29/72